AN AMBIGUOUS BLISS OF BEING BLIND

A play in one scene

Written by

Matt Cav

Copyright 2005 by Matt Cav
cavlit@hotmail.com

ISBN: **1-933704-00-4**

Published by **Redburn Press**
Suite 1102 | 27 West 20th Street | New York, NY 10011

Note from the Publisher

Matt Cav's play, An Ambiguous Bliss of Being Blind came to be published, like many works, in a very roundabout way. E-mail me and I'll tell you the whole story but suffice it to say here that the play was sent to an entertainment lawyer through me with a copy of a release that Matt had signed. Matt had signed this form in order to "hold a meeting" with a famous actor-producer who was interested in producing the play. The release was only to protect the famous actor-producer. But I now had a copy of Matt's play.

Then I read it one easy afternoon. The play was short or I might not have even started reading it. I kept reading. It hooked me. It was heightened revealing conversation between two real people while all the while the drama is: will they – he – break apart? Or leave together? Matt has said it is about timing. In more ways than one, I say. And it is about more than that as well as all good plays are.

It works. I am proud to publish it. I hope it is being produced all over. I hope this is the first published work by a soon-famous writer.

Mark Kohut

Without the connection of Mark Moskowitz, great reader and terrific filmmaker — see STONE READER, a movie discovering a "lost" writer — this Redburn book would not be. Without the working eye of Kristy Buchanan at Lulu, this physical book would look worse and without the attention to detail that Nancy Stewart added, this printed play would read 'significantly other' than it does.

The Players:

OLLIE: A man in his early to mid-thirties, handsome, but in a reserved, not immediately noticed sort of way.

SOPHIE: A woman in her mid to late twenties, or possibly older since it is difficult to tell a woman's age these days. She is handicapped. She wears her hair in two separate braids that fall over her shoulders and a round, curved-top safari hat.

A SECURITY GUARD

Stage Directions: As the curtain rises we see a room in the American wing of the Metropolitan Museum of Art. A red, armless marble bench sits center stage and a plain wall stands behind it upstage. A Winslow Homer painting, The Gulf Stream, presumably is on display downstage, but, of course, cannot be seen. Essentially, throughout the play, the audience is the painting.

OLLIE enters left. He comes in slump-shouldered and weary, and almost staggers his way to the marble bench. He sits but doesn't look up at the Homer painting. Instead, he crosses one leg over the other and massages his ankle and calf muscle.

After a moment, SOPHIE enters left, rolling herself in a wheelchair. OLLIE does not notice her presence in the room, but remains focused on his sore legs. SOPHIE wheels to the opposite end of the bench, turns the chair to face the Homer painting, and admires it. SHE appears the complete opposite of OLLIE, smiling and lighthearted. SHE continues admiring the painting while OLLIE remains oblivious to her presence.

SOPHIE: Do you know why I love this piece?

OLLIE: (Startled) Jesus Christ.

SOPHIE: Oh, I'm sorry, I didn't mean to freak you out. It's funny, though. I did not think I was able to sneak up on anyone anymore, you know, with the squeak-squeak and all... So, do you want to know?

OLLIE: I beg your pardon?

SOPHIE: About the painting - why I like it.

(For the first time OLLIE realizes there is a painting on the wall in front of him and he regards it, but appears indifferent)

OLLIE: Sure. Hit me.

SOPHIE: I love it because it's ... threatening.

OLLIE: Threatening? It looks hopeless to me.

SOPHIE: That's only surface value, a red herring for the novices who come by and say `Oh well, he's fucked'. I'm sorry, I don't mean you're stupid ... But look at him, he's reclined, his legs stretched out, but it's his face - brave if not defiant. And, he's still got his boat.

OLLIE: But look at the boat, the mast has been broken off. He's just riding the waves in the middle of the Gulf -

SOPHIE: (Overlaps) You mean the ocean.

OLLIE: What? Isn't the title "Gulf of Mexico?"

SOPHIE: "The Gulf Stream." The Gulf of Mexico is a large body of water enclosed by land, while the Gulf Stream on the other hand-

OLLIE: (Overlaps) I know what the Gulf Stream is... Look, all I'm saying is that what you call defiant, I think is resignation to the fact that he's - `fucked' - as you said.

SOPHIE: I'm sorry, are you a Jesus freak or something? You know, no GD this, no GD that. I didn't mean to offend you with my language.

OLLIE: Relax, you didn't offend me. I found it fucking refreshing.

SOPHIE: I think people cuss too much. Is it cuss or curse?

OLLIE: I don't think it matters. The only time I hear people say curse is in the movies or written in the Post. In real life everyone says cuss.

SOPHIE: That's what I thought.

>   (Footsteps are heard offstage. SOPHIE and OLLIE glance toward the door expectantly. A SECURITY GUARD enters left, nods, and walks behind the marble bench upstage before turning, walking back, and exits. OLLIE returns to massaging his leg.)

SOPHIE: You seem awfully concerned with your leg. Cramps? Some rare muscular disease?

OLLIE: What? No, I've just been here a long time and my feet are sore. This place seems endless, like I'm trapped in The Vatican or something.

SOPHIE: Ah, so you're not an art admirer.

OLLIE: I didn't say that.

SOPHIE: Of course you did. You said, `this place seems endless', which if you were truly interested you would have followed it with a statement that you'd lifted from a review you read before coming, something exotic and superfluous like: This place seems endless, a phantasmagoria of visual delight, an imaginative maze starting with the beginning of man and carrying us all the way through the Post-modern resurrection of recognition, continually traveling between genius and insanity, a delicious plunge into the creative spirit. How was that? You, on the other hand, said that you felt `trapped', as if lost in The Vatican, which tells me you don't care much for art and possess a deeply rooted resentment against organized religion, probably originating in your late teens and now hidden beneath a veil of nonchalance.

OLLIE: Don't you think all that is a bit presumptuous elicited from one comment? You studying to be a shrink? (beat) First of all, I'm an avid collector, and secondly, I'm a devout Catholic.

SOPHIE: (Bursting into laughter) You're no more a devout anything than I am an Olympic long jumper, and I bet the only piece of art you've collected is a painted rock you saw at a flea market and, for some reason you can't explain, you thought it was cute and would make a good paperweight - although you don't need a paperweight, because, after all, who really needs a paperweight - and you never got around to putting it on your desk and now you don't even know where it is. No, you were forced to come here, probably dragged by someone.

OLLIE: Are you some sort of Svengali?

SOPHIE: You mean a soothsayer?

OLLIE: What's a soothsayer?

SOPHIE: One who foretells things to come, or can sometimes see past events. Svengali is actually a fictional character, created by - was it George or Daphne du Maurier? Anyway, Svengali uses hypnosis to transform a hapless woman into a famous singer.

But after he does this, he holds the girl under his spell and she can't remember her past, and for the rest of the story she's trying to break away from his control. Today the name Svengali has become a metaphor for someone who can control another person's will or actions.

(They pause for a moment and stare at the painting)

So ... what color was your rock?

OLLIE: (Still staring at painting) Yellow with a red circle drawn on the top.

(A long pause ensues. OLLIE drops the leg he has been massaging and raises the other one and begins rubbing while SOPHIE turns and stares at him)

SOPHIE: You know, I can work those cramps out for you.

OLLIE: Excuse me?

(SOPHIE rolls the wheelchair to the other end of the bench, lifts OLLIE'S leg onto her lap and begins massaging. OLLIE reclines on the bench)

SOPHIE: So ... who made you come to the Met? Mother? Father? A homosexual friend?

OLLIE: No, ah, a girl.

SOPHIE: A girl? Are you sure about that?

(OLLIE nods)

Would this be a grown girl or a little girl?

OLLIE: Well, she's short.

SOPHIE: I see. (beat) Well you don't have to worry about being upset if she walks in and sees another woman holding your leg. Since I've been like this I've noticed other women don't seem to look at me like much of a threat.

OLLIE: You're still attractive. I mean your face...

(SOPHIE stops massaging, suddenly resigned, and lifts his leg off her lap. SHE wheels herself back to the other end of the bench. A long pause)

SOPHIE: What do you suppose it's like?

OLLIE: What?

SOPHIE: Being alone on a boat - and not just in a river or a pond, but like him, in the ocean, way out where no one can find you. Well, they used not to be able to find you.

OLLIE: I don't know. I suppose it would be peaceful at first. Then I think, after a storm or something, it would feel ... precarious. Then, I think you'd get lonely.

SOPHIE: I wouldn't be lonely. He doesn't look lonely.

OLLIE: He also doesn't look scared. One of the sharks is almost on the deck and he's not even looking at it.

SOPHIE: Maybe he's seeing something else, perhaps another boat, something Homer wanted us to imagine.

OLLIE: Maybe Winslow Homer couldn't paint frightened faces.

SOPHIE: That's the extent of your criticism? Sometimes I don't know why I talk to you.

OLLIE: We've had a five-minute relationship.

SOPHIE: So you do consider this a relationship?

OLLIE: I...I...I don't know what you mean. I mean I don't know what you want.

(SOPHIE wheels herself behind the bench, behind and around OLLIE, and then parks beside him, facing him)

SOPHIE: Do you know I can still have sex?

OLLIE: What!

SOPHIE: Yeah, a lot of people wouldn't know that, but you - I mean a man - could still do it to me, it can't hurt me. You - the man - would have to use a lubricant -

OLLIE: (Overlaps) What are you talking about?

SOPHIE: (After a beat) Relax. I'm just messing with you.

(SOPHIE turns the wheelchair toward the painting)

OLLIE: ...Have you?

SOPHIE: Have I what?

OLLIE: You know...

SOPHIE: Have I - ever been to Hershey, Pennsylvania?

OLLIE: (Sheepishly) Forget it.

SOPHIE: (After a moment) What do you think happened?

OLLIE: When?

SOPHIE: To the mast?

OLLIE: (Still pouting) It broke off.

SOPHIE: Duh...but how?

OLLIE: (Now looking at the painting) Probably in a storm. I mean look at all the ropes hanging off the boat, the sail probably got tangled and then the weight and the wind made the mast snap.

SOPHIE: Then wouldn't the sail have gone down with the mast?

OLLIE: Yeah, I suppose.

SOPHIE: Then why is it on the deck? See, right there beside the broken stump.

OLLIE: Hm...I don't know. Maybe the mast was already broken off when he got the boat. Maybe he stole it.

SOPHIE: Why? - because he's black?

OLLIE: (Irritated) No. Why is it no one can make an observation anymore because of someone's color, or sex? If that was a white guy on the boat and I said maybe he stole it, you wouldn't have said anything, you might even have agreed with me. But I say maybe he stole it, and because he's black, you come at me like I just made some racist comment.

SOPHIE: Well, I don't know you all that well, how do I know you're not a racist ... or a homosexual?

OLLIE: I told you I was here with a woman!

SOPHIE: What - gay guys don't hang out with women?

OLLIE: I guess.

SOPHIE: (Deadpan) So you are gay.

OLLIE: (Agitated) No!

(The GUARD suddenly enters, standing upstage and staring at the duo to make sure a fight hasn't started. After a moment HE exits)

SOPHIE: (After a pause) Besides, you didn't say you were here with a woman, you said you were here with a `girl', a short girl I believe. It could be a child.

OLLIE: Well, she's not a child. She's a woman.

SOPHIE: But she is younger than you, and by more than a few years I bet.

OLLIE: (Clearly not wanting to talk about it) Goddamn - questions! (HE stands abruptly and walks behind the bench upstage, then turns toward her) Who are you here with?

SOPHIE: (Softly) You.

OLLIE: Stop playing games; you know what I mean. Who did you come in here with?

(Through the following exchanges SOPHIE rolls the wheelchair toward OLLIE, but he keeps moving away from her and they go in a circle around the bench)

SOPHIE: I came in with this.

OLLIE: (Looking over his shoulder at her as he moves) With what?

SOPHIE: With my chair.

OLLIE: That's not what I meant.

SOPHIE: What did you mean?

OLLIE: You know damn well what I meant. Who did you come with?

SOPHIE: I came with all the people who are here.

OLLIE: You're just playing word games with me now.

SOPHIE: You're the one who asked.

OLLIE: (Frantic) I asked if you came with a man!

> (SOPHIE suddenly stops chasing him. The wheelchair is now in front of the bench. OLLIE stops upstage once he realizes she is no longer pursuing him. Slowly HE walks back downstage and stands in front of her)

SOPHIE: (With her head bowed) That's not what you said ... that's not what you asked.

OLLIE: (Hesitant) Well, it's what I meant.

SOPHIE: (Looking up at him) Why do you want to know? (They stare at each other for a moment but OLLIE does not answer her) Are you going to sit back down? (OLLIE sits on the end of the bench) Thank you. I don't like people standing over me, it makes me feel short and I wasn't that short when I used to be able to stand. (Changing gears) You know, when I jumped, I didn't think of anything ... nothing at all ... absolutely no consequences - I mean, who would? I've always found that funny; you would have thought anyone under the circumstances would have thought of the consequences. After all, there are - or were - so many.

OLLIE: When you jumped?

SOPHIE: People jump into things all the time. We like to think of ourselves as so reasoning, so analytical, but, when you think about it, we're not that way at all. We jump into everything, all the time: love, war, sex, hatred, a deal, a trifecta. It doesn't matter – we leap... just like I leapt.

(SOPHIE rolls the wheelchair downstage center, nearly against the audience and tilts her head studying the painting, almost as if hypnotized by it) Have you ever jumped?

OLLIE: To be honest - I have no freaking idea what you're talking about.

SOPHIE: (Still studying painting) I'm talking about jumping ... leaping ... going over the edge and doing something so stupid that, after you've done it, you wonder why you didn't die?

OLLIE: I think I'm starting understand where you're going. (beat) Let me see ...I know one thing that immediately comes to mind, but I've never told anyone. It's more than embarrassing, some people might look at it the wrong way.

(This snags SOPHIE'S interest. SHE backs the wheelchair upstage next to OLLIE, close)

SOPHIE: Well, lay it on me.

OLLIE: (Excited, wanting to tell) This was a long time ago, ten or fifteen years. I was a bit wilder when I was young, I know it sounds cliché, but - hell, who's not? I got into a little trouble, nothing big, just trespassing into a park that closed after dark and drinking with a girl I was kind of seeing. Anyway, some cop with a junior G-man badge rolls in and gives us a ticket. In court the judge assigned me to fifteen hours community service and said the charge would then be tossed out. I had a couple months to complete the community service, but it was summertime, and I was lazy and didn't get around to doing it. I had to go back to court, but I wasn't worried, I thought the judge would just fine me. Well, naturally I get a real tight ass, and after making up some bullshit excuse, the judge shakes his head and sentences me to thirty days in jail. Well, of course, I freak out, and I start rambling and telling him I'll lose my job and so on. So he softens a little and says I can serve my sentence on the weekends. I didn't know anything about jail, but that sounded a hell of a lot better than serving it straight through. Anyway, I do a couple of weekends, but then a problem arose on the third weekend I was supposed to report to lockup. Well, somehow, my friend's father came up with Pirates tickets - I'm from Crafton, a town just outside of Pittsburgh - and the Pirates were playing the Braves in the National League Championship Series and the game was on Saturday night. Well, our beloved Pirates don't get to the playoffs all that often, and it was an opportunity, at the time, I thought was worth any risk. I don't even remember how we came up with it, but it was the stupidest plan and I'm pretty sure it was my concoction. (HE stands and paces in front of the bench as he explains) I figure I can get out of my weekend appointment, so to speak, if I'm injured - you know, like they'll excuse my absence and let me make it up later. But it had to be believable, something so bad they wouldn't dare expect me to report to the jail on Friday night. So, on Thursday night, my friend and the girl I was seeing came over to my place and brought a case of beer and an aluminum baseball bat. The plan was to get me drunk enough to where I wouldn't feel the pain. You see, I told my friend to hit me in the leg with the bat, then I would go outside and lie down in the street and the girl I was dating would start screaming, loud enough for the neighbors to hear it and wake up, and when the ambulance came she would tell them I got hit by a car. Well, if that wasn't bad enough, I came up with something even more farfetched to make myself look like a hero. I told her to tell them that the reason I was in the middle of the street was to save a dog that was about to get hit by the car. She was to tell them I kicked the dog out of the way, which would also explain why I wasn't injured more badly. You know, my body would be in the air from kicking like this, so I would land on the hood of the car and then roll off. Now, there would have to be a car, right. So, we decided to make it a hit-and-run, and I told her to make the details indistinct - a brown car, four doors, American, but older, like from the early eighties. I start drinking around eight o'clock, and by midnight I've got around eighteen beers in me. I'm pretty wobbly by this point and I'm afraid if I drink anymore I'll pass out. So I tell my friend to hit me sometime in the next half-hour - but I tell him not to let me know when he's going to do it cause I'm afraid I'll chicken out. I thought he was going to wait awhile before he did it, so I was relaxed and decided to go to the kitchen and grab another beer. As I turned the corner out of the living room - BAM! - my friend nails me with a home run swing right here in the middle of my thigh. I remember screaming `Holy shit, I didn't know you were going to hit me that hard!' and he said, `You said it had to look real'. Well I buckle and fall on the floor immediately and my leg is in some kind of shock where it's stinging but not hurting yet, like when your foot falls asleep. It isn't until I try to stand up and then fall again that the pain hits, and I realize I should've drunk something stronger than beer. Eventually, with the help of my friend and the girl, I'm able to walk, or rather, limp around. So the girl and me go outside, and I lie down in the street, (HE lies on the floor in front of the bench) and she starts screaming. I remember I started laughing because she sounded so convincing, really panicked and distraught. I didn't know she had it in her - she even faked tears. I start laughing as I'm lying on the street, and in between screams and sobs she's whispering to me to shut the fuck up. It all happened so fast I couldn't believe it. Lo and behold, the first car to come along was, naturally, a patrol car. The girl steps over me and starts waving her arms frantically and the cop screeches to a halt and jumps out. Now I'm having to lie there and pretend I'm unconscious, like this. I can tell the cop is kneeling over me and then I hear him talking to dispatch to send an ambulance and the girl is rambling frantically about this fake hit-and-run driver and the cop is trying to get her to calm down and shut up, and by now my friend has come down to the street to pretend to find out what's going on and the girl is explaining to him and I'm suppressing laughter. It seems like only a second or two later the ambulance arrived and then all hell broke loose. Now I really have to act to fool the EMS unit, trying to make them believe I'm out of it, in some kind of shock or something. I remember hearing a lot of noise, and the EMS guys are pulling up my eyelids and shining a flashlight into my eyes to see whatever. I figure that's going to be it, right, that they'll tie down my head and put me on the stretcher and I'll be off to the hospital where they'll probably keep me overnight. (Now HE stands and sits on the end of the bench near SOPHIE, and speaks with animated gestures) But what I hadn't counted on were the tubes - oh god, I can still feel the pain where they ran the tubes up my nostrils and down into my throat. One should really be unconscious when they do such a thing. Eventually they tie me down on the stretcher and I got tubes running all into me and they put me into the back of the ambulance. I still got my eyes closed because I'm trying to act as unconscious as possible, the way I imagine someone would be after getting hit by a car, but I can hear the EMS workers talking and they're not buying it. I remember them saying how much I stunk like a drunk - from the eighteen beers I'd consumed so I could get hit by the bat - and they're debating on whether I drunkenly stumbled into the street in front of a car or if I didn't get hit at all. All right, this freaks me a bit because I'm worried now that they are going to be able to prove I made it up or shake it out of the girl or my friend, but I decide to stick to my guns, you know, and keep acting hurt. I don't remember what happened when we got to the hospital or what happened the rest of the night. (HE takes a pause to catch his breath) Now, the next day I wake up and I'm in a private room, and I've got an IV running into my arm. The doctor came in, checked on me and asked how I was feeling and he seemed nice enough, so I figure I'm in the clear. Then, he tells me I have visitors. I figure it's my family, but my friend and the girl come into the room - and now is when my real problem comes up.

SOPHIE: (Into the story) They confessed, didn't they?

OLLIE: Nope...my friend comes and stands over me, his hands in his pockets and his eyes keep flickering toward the door to make sure no one is there. In a real low voice he whispers to me, 'They got him'. I ask him, 'Got who?'. And he says, 'The guy driving the car'. All right, now I figure I've entered some parallel universe where I actually must've been hit by a car, bad karma or something, and I say, 'What the hell are you talking about?'. Then he tells me, 'Last night, remember we told the cops an old brown car hit you and sped off, well right around the corner from your place a drunk driver had run off the road and passed out in his seat - he was driving an old, dirty, beat up, brown car - and it even had skid marks across the hood'. I'm so shocked I almost forget to keep acting and I nearly fall out of the bed. I say, 'You've got to be kidding me', and then I tell my friend to tell the cops it wasn't the car and he says they've already done that, but the cops want to hear it from me ...I mean what are the fucking chances? I fake this over the top hit- and-run, and some poor Jack passes out around the corner driving our imaginary car.

SOPHIE: What happened?

OLLIE: Nothing.

SOPHIE: What do you mean?

OLLIE: Some cop comes and questions me, but I tell him I can't remember anything except I think my friends were wrong, that I was pretty sure the car was black, not brown. The cop was pissed because he wanted to nail this guy, but I couldn't let someone go to jail for something I made up and without my corroboration they couldn't pin anything on him. Yeah, so I think that may have been the stupidest thing I've ever done.

SOPHIE: But it worked. They obviously thought a car hit you and you got to go to the Pirates game.

OLLIE: (Shaking his head) Nope...the doctor made me stay for another night for observation. Not only did I not get to go to the game, but I didn't even get to see it. I had the TV on in my room, but about fifteen minutes before the first pitch a nurse comes in and gives me a needle shot in the ass for the pain in my leg, which by now had this gigantic purplish-brown bruise covering my entire thigh. It was Demerol - I was out like a light in ten minutes and I woke up about four hours later as the announcers were summarizing the game.

SOPHIE: So all that for nothing ... unbelievable. But the Pirates won?

OLLIE: No. They lost by one run and the Braves went on to the World Series instead of us. It's funny, I feel like I let the team down, that if I could've at least seen the game we would have won. I know it sounds silly.

SOPHIE: No. I know what you mean.

OLLIE: So do you think differently of me now? I mean having been in jail and coming up with this elaborate hoax to go see a game?

SOPHIE: I think it's ... commendable.

OLLIE: (After a slight pause) Well - it's your turn.

SOPHIE: My turn for what?

OLLIE: The dumbest thing that you've done.

SOPHIE: (Shakes her head) Mine ... (withdraws) Mine are too many to list.

OLLIE: Oh come on -just name one.

SOPHIE: I once provoked a conversation with an ex-con at an art museum.

OLLIE: Nice ... very nice. No, really, tell me one -

SOPHIE: (Overlaps) Do you have any pets?

OLLIE: No.

SOPHIE: No? Not even a goldfish?

OLLIE: No, I'm not answering any more questions until you answer one, one about yourself, anything at all.

SOPHIE: But there's not much to me. It's not like I can be too adventurous in this contraption.

OLLIE: Bullshit. Stop patronizing. (Trying to be somewhat funny) Have you ever fallen out of it?

SOPHIE: That's a rather crude thing to say.

OLLIE: It was a joke. Oh, I see, you can make fun of your... predicament, but I can't. I'm beginning to see why you don't have a man in your life.

SOPHIE: (Offended) Who said I didn't have a man in my life?

OLLIE: Because you wouldn't be here talking to me if you did.

SOPHIE: Well you've got a girl and you're talking to me.

OLLIE: That's different.

SOPHIE: How so?

OLLIE: Because you are the one who talked to me first.

SOPHIE: I didn't see you get up and leave. You didn't walk away.

OLLIE: How can I? You want let anybody. Just when normal pauses come to end a conversation and to say something like 'It was nice talking to you', you come up with another question or another little hypothesis on this goddamn painting, or something even more ludicrous like telling me you could still be fucked (OLLIE stops suddenly, knowing he has gone too far and wishing he could take the words back into his mouth. SOPHIE lowers her head, dejected, and turns the wheelchair away from him.) I didn't mean...

SOPHIE: (Wounded) Yes you did. When anyone says they didn't mean something, they have just told you exactly what they really feel. Please, go away and leave now.

OLLIE: (After a beat) I don't want to.

(There is a tense pause between them. OLLIE keeps looking at her, wondering if she'll speak to him again. SOPHIE keeps her head lowered and the back of the wheelchair facing him)

SOPHIE: (Almost in a whisper) I've got a man, by the way. Well, sort of.

OLLIE: (Stepping lightly) Oh ... what do you mean?

SOPHIE: Nothing really. We used to be together somewhat. Not even that really. I was more like a three a.m. booty call. I don't sleep much, and he always knew I'd be available if he didn't have any luck in the clubs. (Now turns the chair back toward him)

Can you imagine that? - a paraplegic booty call? Who you going to brag to about that? It's like having a midget on the side. I'm sorry, that was a horrible thing to say. Anyway, somewhere along the way I guess he got tired of having a girl that could only lay on her back, or either he found someone else who didn't sleep much. Now he just comes by from time to time in the evening, like when gets off work, and we'll have a few drinks, maybe smoke a little, but that's about it.

OLLIE: It's hard these days, I know.

SOPHIE: I don't see how you can say that, unless you've got a crippling shyness or something. Look at now, I hit on you and you didn't have to say anything, and if I could stand you would be thinking about taking me home with you, and ... I'd agree.

OLLIE: (Hesitant) Are you -

SOPHIE: I...I can't - (OLLIE can't figure out if she's trying to seduce him or is simply being flirtatious) Oh come on, don't be so boyish. If I were able to walk, and I had come in here wearing a tight black miniskirt, and maybe some type of top that squeezed my tits together, are you telling me you wouldn't think about sleeping with me? And I'm not saying it like it's some male chauvinistic thing, women think the same way when we see a guy with a cute face and a nice ass. The funny thing is, men now seem to forget I still have all the same parts underneath here.

OLLIE: Listen: are you trying to hit on me?

SOPHIE: You think that highly of yourself?

OLLIE: (Utterly confused) But you said - (Now angry) Or are you just waiting for him to come by for drinks this evening?

SOPHIE: He's not my boyfriend.

(OLLIE stands and walks a few steps away from the bench with his back turned to SOPHIE)

OLLIE: (To himself) Jesus Christ... (Now turning to SOPHIE) Exactly what are you trying to do to me?

SOPHIE: I'm not trying to do anything to you. I'm merely stating observations you refuse to admit.

OLLIE: I haven't refused anything - (HE moves toward her aggressively, pointing at his heart) I'm not the one who caused what happened to you. It's not my fault!

SOPHIE: (Angrily) Then why are you so worked up?

OLLIE: What are you talking about? You keep saying little comments like you want me to get under your skirt; to lift you off that chair and do whatever, but then I ask -

SOPHIE: (Overlaps) You only ask what you already know. Men do that ... they fish. That's what you are - a fisherman.

OLLIE: And what are you? Huh? Hiding behind your - (Stops himself before going too far)

SOPHIE: Yeah, that's why you're mad. You're not angry because I won't say outright that I might be attracted to you. No, you're pissed because you've got a hard-on for a woman who can't do it to you; who can't do whatever your present flame doesn't do or do that well, either. (Mocking him) If only she could get on her knees, roll over, even bend over instead of lying there like a spread-leg stiff.

OLLIE: (Retreats a step) You're warped.

SOPHIE: Am I? Then why are you backing off?

(OLLIE exhales and drops his head, exhausted. After a moment, HE walks slowly forward and sits on the opposite end of the bench)

OLLIE: I don't even know how we got off on this. I thought we were talking about the painting.

SOPHIE: (Looking at the painting) The painting is just a catalyst. It stimulates a conversation between two people, and in our case, between two strangers who have gotten to know each other.

OLLIE: You don't know anything about me.

SOPHIE: I know you left your girlfriend, that you ran away, or you're trying to run away. It's like a test, a little rehearsal. If you can just get away from her for a little while in the museum, to lose her for a few minutes, then maybe next time you walk out the door you can stay away a bit longer, and then the time you walk out after that maybe it can be permanent. I've seen how people leave, each person does it a small bit in their own way, but eventually all break-ups become the same. That voice in the back of your head: run, run, run away. And then there's another voice in there: you can't do that to her, not today, maybe tomorrow. But you're scared and you wait for someone, someone who'd give you a reason to leave. A security blanket.

OLLIE: I just got separated from her in the Modern Art wing.

SOPHIE: Modern Art? That's all the way at the other end of the building. I think if you wanted to be found, at least by her, you would have stayed somewhere down there instead of finding the farthest point away from her without leaving the museum completely.

OLLIE: I'm glad you've got your life all figured out.

SOPHIE: We're not talking about my life.

OLLIE: No, of course not, what would happen then?

SOPHIE: (After a beat) Ask me a question.

OLLIE: What?

SOPHIE: Ask me a question.

OLLIE: About what?

SOPHIE: (Pleading) Just ask me a fucking question.

OLLIE: Ah...what's you're favorite color?

SOPHIE: Don't have one.

OLLIE: (Exasperated) AHHHHH.

SOPHIE: Now ask me another one.

OLLIE: I don't want to.

SOPHIE: Come on, ask me something else, something less juvenile.

OLLIE: How did it happen?

SOPHIE: I told you, I jumped.

OLLIE: Off a building?

SOPHIE: No. I told you I didn't try to off myself. I don't have any respect for people who commit suicide - it's way too easy to get yourself killed in the city, all they had to do was figure out where to hang for awhile. You know what I like about living here? The hypocrisy. I was in a bar the other day and I overheard this conversation between two men - one was from here and the other was a visitor. So they talked for a few minutes and then the Manhattanite asked the visitor where he came from. The gentleman said he was from the South. You know what the Manhattanite says to him? He says, 'Ah, a redneck. Did you bring your shotgun?' Now, I figure the visitor is about to knock this city dweller into another borough, but instead he lifts a copy of the New York Post off the bar. For the next half-hour he reads aloud forty-seven articles about people being shot in the city, eleven of which were fatal, and all occurring on one day. When he finishes, the Manhattanite has no comeback, but the visitor has one more trick up his sleeve. He reaches down into his satchel and pulls out a copy of his hometown newspaper. Now this is only a weekly paper and it's still pretty thin. He slams it down on the bar and tells the Manhattanite that this is a record of an entire week in his hometown and that he hasn't read it yet, and wagers $500 if he can find one report of a shooting, much less a homicide. Well, by now the other patrons have heard the conversation and they're laughing at city boy - who's all red in the face now - and instead of making the bet he rolls his eyes and turns away from the visitor to hide his shame. So the Southerner raises his drink to his lips and then says aloud, 'Opossum-breath plebeian'. I burst out laughing and not simply because of the perfectly phrased cutdown. No, I laugh more so because the Manhattanite didn't get it - he didn't know what plebeian meant. How about that. The man who had so originally come up with something so banal as `redneck', couldn't figure out he'd been insulted by `plebeian'. (beat) It made my day.

OLLIE: (Feigning embarrassment) Ah...what ...what does plebeian mean?

SOPHIE: (In disbelief) Ah! Someone who is common, vulgar. (OLLIE starts giggling) You bastard! You knew what it meant all along!

OLLIE: (Still chuckling) If I'm not mistaken it is Latin for common people, the way they separated classes. In Ancient Rome, Plebs were the common people.

SOPHIE: You are a bastard.

OLLIE: (Calming) So you didn't try to kill yourself?

SOPHIE: I told you, it's too easy to get killed in the city without having to worry about doing it yourself.

OLLIE: All right ... you jumped. How long ago?

SOPHIE: Years.

OLLIE: How many? Were you a little girl?

SOPHIE: (Becoming distant) I was younger than I am now.

OLLIE: I don't get it.

SOPHIE: (Still distant) That's because you haven't jumped. (A pause, then she changes gears) When I was a little girl my mother used to take me to the zoo. I never asked to go, but parents assume children want to go; to the zoo, to the circus, to get your face painted. To be honest, the zoo bored me. All those animals, unable to move much, unable to do anything really - except fornicate - and that's just for the lucky ones. Zookeepers are like pimps. I remember how pitiful they looked, staring at each person who came by, and for a brief second you could see the glimmer of hope in their eyes when they first saw me and wondered if I was going to be the one to unlock the cage. But then I'd pass by and their shoulders would drop and they'd go back to trying to remember what they had been thinking...I bet they thought if they could just get out of the cage that they would be home. I bet they never realized that even if they were able to hop the fence that they'd still be thousands of miles from their native land ...I didn't think of it quite the same way as I got older. I started to see them differently, especially the species with the eyes on the sides of their heads. They are prey, and from the moment they are born they are meant to do two things: be killed and be eaten. Cows, fish, chickens, lambs, even horses ... that's their real purpose. But it's the ones with their eyes fixed in the front of their skulls, the predators, I still felt sorry for. Those like us - where our eyes are. They possess a different kind of quality than the prey, an innate understanding of freedom, and what it means to have it taken away. It's in these animals where you see it - the utter acknowledgement of inescapable loss.

(There is a long pause as they digest the gravity of what she has said. The GUARD enters and walks methodically upstage. HE pretends to be performing his usual round, but he is really checking on the duo)

SOPHIE: (In a low voice) How'd you like to make twenty bucks?

OLLIE: What do you mean?

SOPHIE: I'll give you twenty bucks to go over and ask the guard how much he wants for the painting, for this one, The Gulf Stream.

OLLIE: You're out of your mind. He'll think I'm nuts.

SOPHIE: I know. Come on. Twenty dollars.

OLLIE: No.

SOPHIE: You really are chickenshit. You'll never leap. (SOPHIE glares at him briefly and then becomes determined. SHE turns the wheelchair and rolls quickly upstage and stops in front of the GUARD'S feet) Excuse me. My husband - (SHE points to

OLLIE) wanted to know how much you want for that one, (Points to painting) the Winslow Homer.

GUARD: (Vexed) Ah... ah, lady, this is the Metropolitan Museum of Art. Nothing is for sale here. Winslow Homer is one of America's most known artists. You can purchase a print of this piece downstairs in the gift shop.

SOPHIE: A print! What am I going to do with a print?

OLLIE: (Embarrassed) Um, Honey, don't you think you should come back here?

SOPHIE: No - dear - not until he makes me a fair offer.

GUARD: (Slightly irritated) This is a museum.

(The GUARD turns and walks away. SOPHIE pursues a bit behind him)

SOPHIE: (Calling out to the Guard) Fifteen dollars ... Twenty ... Fifty? (The GUARD exits and SHE stops just before going offstage) Are you an immigrant? I can pay in pesos ... kroners ... deutschemark ... yen?

(SHE turns the wheelchair to face downstage, and she is smiling, quite delighted with herself. SHE rolls the chair back to the bench) See. That is how it's done. Did you see the guard's face?

OLLIE: He's probably gone to call for backup. Any minute now we'll be sitting in the middle of the largest SWAT operation in Met history.

SOPHIE: Don't be so melodramatic. Are you really that chickenshit? What happened to the man who faked getting hit by a car to see a baseball game?

OLLIE: He got ... older.

SOPHIE: I don't believe in getting older.

OLLIE: Then you might want to avoid your reflection during the upcoming decades.

SOPHIE: I don't mean the body, physical aging. I'm talking about in here. (Points to her head) I think adults are just children who can drive. (SHE rolls her wheelchair back and forth) I'm not sure I'm that much different than I was when I was a girl.

OLLIE: Then you must not have had much pain in your life.

SOPHIE: (Motioning toward her legs) ...Hello...

OLLIE: I'm sorry, I didn't mean ...I was talking about myself, really. I don't even remember what I thought as a child.

SOPHIE: That bad, huh. Well, can you remember what you thought as an adult? What you thought this morning? What you want?

OLLIE: (Shrugging) Same as anyone else, I guess. No, wait, that's not true ...I don't remember. I don't think about it anymore. I don't know why. It just seems the morning comes and before I know it, it is night. I've never realized it, at least not recently. I suppose you could say I've been shuffling. You know, being alive merely for the sake of being alive. No, it's not that dramatic - I don't think about my dreams slipping away or anything like that - it's simply sort of...

SOPHIE: Dulled senses?

OLLIE: Perhaps.

SOPHIE: What about the girl in Modern Art? Do you plan to marry her someday?

OLLIE: (Halfheartedly laughing) No - I'll never marry again.

SOPHIE: Ah, so you have taken a leap before. I wouldn't have expected it from you. What was your marriage like?

OLLIE: Hiroshima at first. Then it became Nagasaki.

SOPHIE: How long have you been holding on to that answer, waiting for someone to ask?

OLLIE: (Smiling) A few years.

SOPHIE: Well. What happened?

OLLIE: (Stands up, fidgety) I need a drink. Aren't you thirsty? I believe I saw a café, a restaurant or something downstairs. I wonder if they serve cocktails? At least a beer.

SOPHIE: Why are you trying to run away?

OLLIE: I'm not trying to run away. I'm thirsty. It's a natural human function. (OLLIE tries to move toward the exit, but SOPHIE blocks his way)

SOPHIE: What are you doing?

OLLIE: I'm going down to get a drink.

SOPHIE: You can't.

OLLIE: Why not?

SOPHIE: I'm not thirsty.

OLLIE: Look, I can get around that wheelchair... We were going to have to say goodbye sooner or later.

SOPHIE: Do we?

OLLIE: Do we what?

SOPHIE: Say goodbye?

OLLIE: (Retreating) Listen, I'll go down and get a drink, and if I don't bump into -

SOPHIE: (Overlaps) If you don't bump into her you'll come back up? (SHE turns the wheelchair away from him) Go. Go get your drink. (Doubtfully) I'm sure you'll be right back.

(There is a pause as SOPHIE keeps her back turned to OLLIE, but occasionally tries to steal glances to see if he has decided. OLLIE is tired, anxious, and uncertain)

OLLIE: You know (beat) you... could come down with me.

SOPHIE: (Turning chair around toward him) Could I? And what would we do if we bumped into her?

OLLIE: Well - (Thinks about it)- we haven't done anything, nothing that's wrong.

SOPHIE: I think she would see through that.

OLLIE: See through what?

SOPHIE: Your tone. You make it sound like you're trying to cover up something.

OLLIE: Oh, really. And where did we go? What did I do, wheel you out of the museum, got a cab, got a room, and then rushed back here?

SOPHIE: We could have bonked in the bathroom stall. Or we could do something simpler. Perhaps kiss?

OLLIE: (After consideration) Do?

SOPHIE: Excuse me?

OLLIE: You said `do', not we did. You didn't make it into a hypothetical.

SOPHIE: I didn't?

OLLIE: No, you didn't.

SOPHIE: Huh.

(OLLIE takes a step closer to her, forgetting about the drink, but stops short and slowly, hesitantly sits on the bench near her. They stare at each other for a moment, about to or about not to)

OLLIE: (Awkwardly) Where, where do you live?

SOPHIE: Why?

OLLIE: (Cowers and the moment passes) Um, it's just one of those questions. Where do you live, what do you do for a living, so on. Wait - what do you do for a living?

SOPHIE: I live alone. I have an apartment downtown, more of a flat really. I've been meaning to get a T.V. I know, it sounds absurd that someone doesn't have a television these days, but I'm out a lot and I still have mounds of books in my place I haven't read.

That's one of my fears, one of my quirks: I'm terrified I'll die before I get a chance to read them all.

OLLIE: I'm afraid I'll die before I get a chance to go to North Dakota.

SOPHIE: North Dakota? What's in North Dakota?

OLLIE: I have no idea, that's one of the reasons I want to go. Everybody always talks about their posh vacations. Oh, we spent a week in Acapulco, Miami, Rome, Thailand. No one ever says they went on a wonderful getaway to North Dakota, though. I thought it would be funny, standing around the water cooler at work or at a bar, listening to everyone talking about their beaches and other continents and when they ask me I tell them they haven't been anywhere until they go to North Dakota.

SOPHIE: You are really a complex man, aren't you?

OLLIE: ...Not really.

SOPHIE: What do you think is possible?

OLLIE: How so?

SOPHIE: Do you marry the woman you love or do you keep the woman you love as your mistress? (OLLIE breaks into laughter) What?

OLLIE: That just sounds so ... British.

SOPHIE: (Obstinate) I think it's Russian. Pasternak. Yuri and Lara and Yuri's wife. Tolstoy. Anna Karenina and Vronsky. You've never read Anna Karenina or Doctor Zhivago?

OLLIE: I've seen the movie. I had a crush on Julie Christie when I was a child.

SOPHIE: Really? Why?

OLLIE: Same reason as Yuri Zhivago.

SOPHIE: I see. And would you have chosen the same as Zhivago, to not get in the sled with Rod Stieger and Julie Christie, to not come to the train station?

OLLIE: (Heavy) I don't know.

SOPHIE: What do you suppose it's like falling in love once you're already obligated to someone else?

(OLLIE glares quickly at SOPHIE, as if seeing through her)

OLLIE: (Firmly) I don't know.

(OLLIE rises off the bench slowly and gradually walks upstage and stops with his back turned to the audience. After a moment SOPHIE addresses him, but she does not turn to look at him)

SOPHIE: So what was Hiroshima like? Did Nagasaki leave you or did you leave her?

OLLIE: (Turning around, staring blankly) I'm not sure.

(SOPHIE still doesn't turn around and face him for the following questions)

SOPHIE: Did you hit her?

OLLIE: No.

SOPHIE: Did you tell her you didn't love her?

OLLIE: No. As a matter of fact, I think I said it too many times.

SOPHIE: How is that possible?

OLLIE: Pleading.

SOPHIE: Ah, so it was she who left you?

OLLIE: I didn't say it then, at least not when she left for good.

SOPHIE: She left more than once?

OLLIE: Many times.

SOPHIE: Why?

OLLIE: To go fuck other men.

SOPHIE: (Slowly) Oh. (beat) She met someone?

OLLIE: No. Yes. No, not really. (OLLIE paces slowly back and forth upstage as he speaks) She had a disease. I guess you would call it a disease. She couldn't be monogamous, at least not physically monogamous. When we got married she told me she'd only been with a few men... it turned out to be more than a few, a lot more. I didn't mind that, truly I didn't, women have a misconception that men don't want to marry someone who's been around. I minded the lie, the really big lie, which led to another and another, and the way I found out, piece by piece. A letter here, a condom wrapper under the bed - we didn't use condoms - a photograph. And then ... well, I thought it was just one person since we'd been together. Then it turned into two. Then it became ten.

SOPHIE: So then you left.

(OLLIE stops pacing and stands upstage center)

OLLIE: No. (beat) People always say they would leave if their spouse cheated, but it doesn't work out that way, not when it really happens.

SOPHIE: So what did happen? How did it end?

OLLIE: Eventually she found a flavor she liked a little more than for just a fling. He had money, and - poof - she was gone.

SOPHIE: I'm sorry. It sounds rough.

OLLIE: (Walking back downstage) It wasn't as bad as I thought it would be, I mean afterwards, after she left. (HE sits on the bench) I realized how much it had killed me while we were together. The waiting. The wondering. The paranoia. But once I realized it was finally over for good, the part about losing her didn't hurt.

SOPHIE: What part did hurt?

OLLIE: It was losing - (HE stops. A long pause) It was nothing. Can we talk about something else for a while?

SOPHIE: (Motioning toward audience) We can go back to the painting.

OLLIE: Oh, yes, our hopeless friend on his raft.

SOPHIE: First of all it's a boat, at least what's left of a boat, and secondly we concluded that he was defiant.

OLLIE: No, no, I don't think I concurred. (Pausing to look at the painting and then something occurs to him) Huh.

SOPHIE: What?

OLLIE: Something we didn't consider. Did it ever dawn on you he might be blind?

SOPHIE: What?

OLLIE: Why not? Maybe that's why he looks so unconcerned – or defiant as you say - because he doesn't know any better. He can't see the sharks or the approaching storm.

SOPHIE: Well don't blind people have heightened senses?

OLLIE: On a boat? And how's he going to sense sharks in the water. They're not wearing Oil of Olay skin cream. No, he's lucky.

SOPHIE: How can being blind be lucky?

OLLIE: Ignorance. Ignorance is bliss. He doesn't know his boat's listing severely and one of the sharks is nearly at his toes.

SOPHIE: That's absurd.

OLLIE: Why? Do you want to know everything that you know?

SOPHIE: Yes ... no ... maybe, I don't know.

OLLIE: Exactly. That's why heaven would absolutely suck.

SOPHIE: Heaven!

OLLIE: Heaven. It's preposterous about a notion of eternal paradise, an infinity without conflict.

SOPHIE: Isn't that what everyone is trying to achieve here? A world without conflicts?

OLLIE: Of course.

SOPHIE: Then how can you say we don't want heaven?

OLLIE: Have you ever seen a movie where someone has everything they want; women, money, palaces, fine foods. (SOPHIE nods) But they're never happy are they? No, suddenly they have to lose it and go on a tumultuous journey before they regain their soul, and in the end, even if they don't possess the multitude of material things they started out with, they become content because they remember who they are and that the journey's the thing.

SOPHIE: That's Homer.

OLLIE: And Homer was on to something in the Odyssey. It's in the struggle that makes an achievement worth anything. Heaven would take that away - the drama. No, the only worthwhile religion I know is football.

SOPHIE: Football?

OLLIE: Yeah, football. And I say football because it is the only team sport where every player on the field has to perform on every play to make a play work. It is the ultimate team sport.

SOPHIE: But what does that have to do with religion?

OLLIE: Are you kidding? It possesses every component of life: love - for your teammates; hate - for the opposition; pain - getting hurt; agony - losing; exaltation - winning; fulfillment for both the individual and the collective good; strategy; politics; arguments; embraces; pushing one's ultimate limits; admiration; cheers; boos; lonely moments in the spotlight; and being carried triumphantly off the field.

SOPHIE: You've given a lot of thought to this.

OLLIE: I have a lot of spare time on my hands.

SOPHIE: I don't believe in heaven, either - at least not what's written. First we believe in Santa Claus, but then we find out he's not real. Then it's the tooth fairy and then the Easter Bunny. Then we find out Captain Kangaroo is just an actor who's now dead. But for some reason people still hold out for Jesus, the peaceful David Koresh of his time. Can you imagine how much credence we'd given Jesus if he'd come along in the Sixties? No, the Bible was written by a bunch of homophobic men, who obviously had a problem holding on to their wives ... Yeah ... (thinking) ...I don't want to go to heaven, either.

OLLIE: Good. Now I'll have someone to hang out with through all eternity.

SOPHIE: What do you suppose we'll do?

OLLIE: I'm sure something will come to mind. (after a beat) Do you want to get a drink?

SOPHIE: Where in the afterlife do you suppose we'll find a pub?

OLLIE: No, no - I meant today ... now.

SOPHIE: You're asking me to go with you to get a drink?

(HE nods)

Here? Downstairs?

OLLIE: We could leave.

SOPHIE: You mean leave the museum, leave the Met? Hmm. And what about shorty in Modern Art?

OLLIE: (Reacts as if he'd forgotten all about her) Oh ... well ... I'm sure she'll be here for hours.

SOPHIE: What if we don't make it?

OLLIE: What do you mean?

SOPHIE: What if we don't make it out? What if she's down there? (SHE motions toward exit) I can't exactly run in this.

OLLIE: What are the chances? Come on, we're talking about getting a drink, not - (Stops awkwardly)

SOPHIE: (Offended) We're not?

OLLIE: Well, no, I mean not yet.

SOPHIE: So there is a possibility? I mean a possibility that it might be something you wish to pursue?

OLLIE: (Uncertain) I...guess so.

SOPHIE: Hmm. (beat) Now, is this a one-time only deal, or am I going to be your secret fucker?

OLLIE: I'm just talking about getting a drink!

SOPHIE: No you're not - you've already admitted you've thought about it.

OLLIE: Thought about it, I haven't acted upon it.

SOPHIE: (As if answering a game show question) Aristotle!

OLLIE: What?

SOPHIE: Aristotle. Aristotle said what a man thought didn't matter whatsoever. All that counted were his actions.

OLLIE: Well, that may be, but I don't think Aristotle was talking about sex.

SOPHIE: How do you know? You don't think Aristotle thought about sex? You don't think he ever did it?

OLLIE: Oh my god - how did we get off on Aristotle?

SOPHIE: Is that supposed to be a pun? Getting off on Aristotle?

OLLIE: (Frustrated) Fine. Whatever. We'll just stay here.

SOPHIE: (After a pause) Are you handicap accessible?

OLLIE: What?

SOPHIE: Your penis? Is it handicap accessible?

OLLIE: (Stands and walks upstage) Now you're just trying to get under my skin.

SOPHIE: Is that another pun?

(OLLIE returns to the bench but remains standing)

OLLIE: What did I do to piss you off?

SOPHIE: You haven't done anything. I'm not pissed at you.

OLLIE: Then why are you playing word games - mind games - with me? I wanted to take you for a drink, but then you start probing into my sexual aspirations, and then as if that's not enough, you seem to want to set up some type of arrangement, like we're plotting... (Suddenly realizing what she wants and speaks softly) to have an affair. (OLLIE sits slowly on the bench) That's it: you don't want a one-night stand.

SOPHIE: I've had plenty of one-night stands.

OLLIE: Had being the key word. You don't want a one-nighter with me; you want an affair.

SOPHIE: Talk about presumptuous.

OLLIE: No, no, don't talk your way around this, admit it.

SOPHIE: How do you know I'm not asking you to leave your girlfriend before I'll sleep with you?

OLLIE: (Very serious) Because you wouldn't take the risk that I might refuse.

(SOPHIE'S disposition changes, being psychologically exposed. SHE rolls the wheelchair downstage, almost to the edge, and speaks without looking at OLLIE)

SOPHIE: (Disconnected) Why can't you be like our friend, why can't you be blind? So you think I'm that cowardly, you think I'll open my legs up for you without asking you to leave her ... and, of course, you think I'll do this because I'm in a wheelchair, that I can't afford to risk that you might say no if I tried to be too noble about it. That's the funny part, because that's where you're wrong. Before I was like this I would have slept with you without asking you to leave her. That is the kind of girl I was - I got around, as people say. I wasn't embarrassed about it; I mean I wasn't the trophy slut. In fact, I was upfront about it. Men speak openly about girls they've done, but it's taboo for a woman to be so frank. So, you see, I realized how fucked up people were before I got fucked up. (SOPHIE rolls the wheelchair back to the bench and faces OLLIE) So ... what do you think of me now?

OLLIE: Honestly? (She nods) I wish I'd have known you before this happened.

SOPHIE: (Resigned) I wish you had, too.

(There is a pause as they return to looking at the painting. After a moment, OLLIE stares at SOPHIE and we can tell he is mustering the courage to ask her a question)

OLLIE: Please, how did it happen? I think we've become close enough for you to tell me.

SOPHIE: I jumped. (OLLIE looks at her plaintively) Okay. It's nothing special. It was a custom, a ritual. I was a senior in high school and it was two days before graduation. One of the senior traditions was going up to a place called Twin Falls on the river that went through our town. It's only one waterfall instead of two, and I don't know where the name came from, but we'd go up on the cliffs and jump into the river. Dozens of senior classes had done it through the years long before I came. It happened on my third jump; I had already gone twice before alone. We chose to go higher up, a little upstream where the cliffs were higher. We jumped and I landed on a rock that was hidden under the river. That was it, no graduation, no party, no summer, and no more leaps. Thousands of seniors had taken that leap, but I chose to do it differently, to go a bit higher and ... when we jump far, we land hard.

OLLIE: We? You said 'we chose to go higher up'. Who were you with?

SOPHIE: ...Nobody. (A long beat) I used to dance - I mean really dance, break-men's-ankles kind of dancing ...I miss it, I miss the way some guys would take me out on the floor thinking they could get by with only moving one leg and rotating in a circle - you know the type of men you see at a club? (OLLIE nods)

Sometimes I felt sorry for them, like the ones who beforehand told me they couldn't dance. Oddly enough, most of those guys were the ones who weren't intimidated, I mean like the way you weren't intimidated by me sleeping with my share of men. But it was the ones who could really dance - and usually they were younger than me - who got scared shitless when I started talking about sex, and although they'd said they'd done this and that, a threesome even, you could tell they were full of it, boys waiting for their first pimple whose only manage a trois had been with their penis, a magazine, and a locked bathroom door. I miss being crazy, being able to be crazy. I think I had two eighteens and went straight into middle-aged.

OLLIE: You're nowhere near middle-aged.

SOPHIE: Not if you go by numbers. But if you go by reality I think I'm about to scoot past it and enter my golden years.

OLLIE: Please! You're the same as you were then, I can tell. You're still crazy. Look at this moment, this conversation, what we've talked about. I would've never done this. You, you started this all.

SOPHIE: There's a difference between crazy and desperation.

OLLIE: Now I think you're full of shit and trying to throw a pity party.

SOPHIE: Did you really just say, `pity party'? You're a grown man and pull that after-school lingo out of your ass? I mean, come on, we were just discussing going to bed together a few minutes ago. (A pause)

OLLIE: (Wanting to return to that subject) Speaking of which ... you never really answered me on that.

SOPHIE: On what?

OLLIE: You know - what we were discussing.

SOPHIE: I don't remember hearing a question.

OLLIE: You know, we were talking and then you were saying what you were like before.

SOPHIE: So?

OLLIE: Well ... are you still the same?

SOPHIE: You mean despite the obvious restriction? You know, if this is how you go about asking a girl if she still sleeps around, you're not going to ever find out. The trick is to make me feel unique, not slutty.

OLLIE: I'm not trying to make you feel like a slut. I mean I don't think you are one. Do you think I'd want to go to bed with you if you were?

SOPHIE: Why not? It's all about appearance. If you were good looking enough and you were just a male gigolo, I'd do you. Promiscuous people are far easier to trust.

OLLIE: All right, you've done it again; you've completely lost me. Did I just get insulted? Did you just tell me I wasn't good looking?

SOPHIE: That depends. If you're a gigolo, then no, you're not good looking enough. But if you're less, hmm, shall we say experienced, then you're plenty good looking.

OLLIE: (Spiraling) What about today? What about at this moment?

SOPHIE: I thought you were only asking me out for a drink?

OLLIE: Huh?

SOPHIE: And besides, did we ever determine if I wanted a one-night stand (or a one-afternoon stand really) or if I wanted the full-blown affair?

OLLIE: I guess that would be up to you.

SOPHIE: Good god, my how quickly we give in. I hope you're not a hostage negotiator, otherwise there'll be big business in the kidnapping genre. Why are you so eager to go to bed with me all of a sudden?

OLLIE: I didn't say I wanted to go to bed with you. We were talking about getting a drink.

SOPHIE: Whoa, whoa chief - you can't slow down once you've already blown the brakes. Don't try to skirt around the issue.

OLLIE: You are telling me not to skirt around an issue - that's all you do!

SOPHIE: I disagree. We wouldn't be talking about becoming involved if I hadn't started talking to you.

OLLIE: And since you have started talking to me that's all you've done. You harp on one subject and then when we reach the crux of the matter you start babbling about something else.

SOPHIE: Babbling! You think I babble?

OLLIE: (Accusatory) No, I don't think you babble, I think you try to get people to put their foot in their mouth. You're like an attorney trying to twist a witness's words and thoughts into some convoluted mess that a jury won't be able to figure out. God! - I don't think you can even tell what you want, but I'll never be able to know that because once somebody just about figures you out, you go and turn all the tables around like some teenage prima donna trying to tease every guy who comes along. You sound more like the girls you say you're not like than the person you say you are!

SOPHIE: (Defensive) Then I can see why you want to fuck me!

OLLIE: (Standing abruptly) I'm not trying to fuck anybody! I wouldn't even know how to fuck you!

(With this comment OLLIE has gone too far. SOPHIE stares at him for a moment and tries to suppress her tears, but after a beat SHE drops her head and begins to slightly weep. OLLIE steps toward her, attempting to console) Wait. I'm sorry, I didn't mean -

SOPHIE: (Beating him off with closed fists) Bullshit! You're so fucking overt. Trying to argue with yourself about whether or not you want to have sex with a cripple, as if I'll just lie down because I should be thankful given my circumstance!

(OLLIE staggers backwards, then regains himself. HE stands still for a moment and watches her weep before becoming assertive again)

OLLIE: Look at you. Look at this. What have you lost? You can't walk - it happens. But do you think you're lucky? Of course you could've died, or you could've been in coma, or completely paralyzed. But no, you want to bitch about your legs and make everyone else like they're out to get something for free. I didn't want to be with you because I thought you had to sleep with me; I wanted you, you the conversationalist, that carefree person who first rolled herself in here. But you're too busy thinking you've lost something.

SOPHIE: (Still regaining herself) And what have you ever lost?

OLLIE: (Suddenly deadly serious) My soul.

(SOPHIE now pauses, raises her head, and looks at him curiously)

SOPHIE: What the hell does that mean?

(OLLIE becomes disconnected as if admitting to a guilt that will condemn him to eternal damnation)

OLLIE: My son. I lost my son.

SOPHIE: Oh. (beat) I'm sorry, I wouldn't have been so -

OLLIE: (Overlaps) Stop ... he's not dead. I just lost him.

SOPHIE: I...I don't understand.

(OLLIE wanders downstage corner, staring off through or past the audience during the following speech)

OLLIE: He was five years old the last time I saw him ... Jesus Christ, he'd be ten now. My wife, my ex-wife, let's call her Mary cause I don't feel like saying her name. It was towards the end, when she started staying with the guy she liked for more than a month. She asked to meet me. I thought we were going to talk about getting back together. It was May, a hot afternoon, and we met at the town square. I remember how cheerful she looked as she approached, vibrant, younger than I had remembered her. I thought the prospect of us reuniting was the fuel for this rebirth. We made idle chitchat for a few minutes and then out of the blue she suddenly blurts out that she's filed for a divorce and that I should be served with the papers any day. Needless to say, I was stunned. Then she just got up and walked away ...I thought I would try to stop her, like I had done before when I said I pleaded, but, for some reason, it wasn't in me anymore. I just sat there, I can't tell you for how long, but I couldn't get up. I don't even remember going home that night. A few days later a deputy served me with the papers and a few days after that I spoke to Mary on the telephone about how this was going to work. She said it had nothing to do with our son, that it wasn't a custody hearing and that she thought we could work it out for ourselves. Our divorce hearing wasn't for another two months, and I simply chose to ignore thinking about it as much as possible. I made a mistake, though ...I allowed myself to be lonely. It's a dangerous thing when someone becomes lonely, it distorts judgment more than alcohol could ever do. (beat) I took a lover - is that how it's said? - it doesn't matter. I felt absolutely nothing for this woman, other than the fact she was there. She was plain looking, older, I think even a few times divorced, but she didn't ask anything of me, and she didn't need me to explain anything to her. I think she was beyond all that. She was smarter. She didn't want to know. It didn't last long, only long enough for Mary to have the fodder she needed ... I'll never figure out how Mary found out ... Anyway, six weeks after that May afternoon, Mary calls and asks to meet me at the same place again. Can you believe I was stupid enough to again think that it was about getting back together? This time she looked different, less vibrant and more on a mission. I knew as soon as I saw her that this wasn't going to be about getting back together. She was walking in that way she walked when she thought she was more important than anyone, a manner I can't put into words but you would know if you saw her. Here she had had over a dozen affairs that I knew about since we'd been married, but leave it to Mary to be the one to pull out photographs. I know it was her idea to hire an investigator - she thought that way - and I know the expenses came from the guy she was now living with. It didn't matter. I remember that shine in her eyes when she told me I was done for, sunk, and to forget about the joint custody she'd dangled in front of my face and said that I'd have to fight to just get mere visitation. It's the only time in my life I knew I could kill someone, I mean really do it. I even dreamt about it a few times later on. Instead, I left. That is when

I moved to New York. I've never gone back. I used to send my son gifts on his birthday and on Christmas, and afterwards I held out hope that I'd have a letter from him. But my mailbox remained empty. I've often thought it would be easier if he had died - I know it sounds horrible - but then I wouldn't know that he's out there. I can't explain to you why I can't go back. If I did I know I wouldn't make it. Late at night, though, I imagine these extravagant plans and I dream, I dream of myself kidnapping him and he's happy again and he asks me to take him away and to never leave again. And I promise, I promise him we'll always be together...

SOPHIE: (After a beat) Have you ever thought about fighting, taking it back to court? Maybe contacting one of the guys Mary did while you were married for a witness?

OLLIE: I couldn't. (Turns and faces SOPHIE) I couldn't.

SOPHIE: Your son probably hates you now. (OLLIE returns upstage and sits on the bench)

OLLIE: I know.

(There is a long pause. OLLIE and SOPHIE are exhausted)

SOPHIE: You're not a murderer.

OLLIE: How's that going to help me?

SOPHIE: You didn't kill your son. You didn't kill someone you loved. You see, I grabbed her.

OLLIE: I'm not in the mood for any more mind games.

SOPHIE: Julie was my best friend. You don't need to know anything more about her other than that. She was one who went up with me. She was the one who jumped off the cliff with me.

Julie also hit the rock, but Julie never got off of it. The impact severed her spinal cord, broke her neck in two places, crushed one lung, broke various other bones, and, oh yeah, officially she died from head trauma. Yeah, so at least you didn't kill anyone.

OLLIE: (Trying to digest this information) But ... neither did you. It wasn't your fault. You didn't kill her.

SOPHIE: (Almost as if not bothered by it) Oh but I did. (Now she fights for the words) You see, we jumped at the same time. It would have been different if Julie had been bigger or smaller than me, if she had been able to fall at a different speed than I fell. But we were side by side on our way down, young, beautiful, everything ...I reached out and grabbed her wrist, and pulled her toward me. But, here's the really heinous part: I knew I was going to hit the rock. Just before, about ten feet above the water's surface, I suddenly saw it, this dark boulder right below the river. I don't know why I did it. I reached out and grabbed Julie's wrist, pulling her body even more off balance and dooming her to hit the rock in that contorted, unprotected way. Yeah, I murdered Julie. I killed my best friend.

OLLIE: (After a long beat) Let's get out of here. Come on, for real, let's just go, let's go anywhere - we could even leave the city.

SOPHIE: Thank you.

OLLIE: For what?

SOPHIE: For not saying any bullshit; for allowing yourself to be surprised. You didn't try to say anything swift, you know, like it was a reflex for me to reach out and grab her.

OLLIE: I figure you got to figure those things out on your own.

SOPHIE: Yeah, I suppose you're right. I'm sorry I had to say something, I mean about your son and what he may be feeling.

OLLIE: No. You only said the truth.

SOPHIE: Yeah, well, sometimes people should lie... (A pause, then SOPHIE sounds upbeat) Let's go, let's really go. We'll get in a car, no - a train - we'll take a train upstate somewhere!

OLLIE: (Excited) We could be at Grand Central in ten minutes!

SOPHIE: What about packing? What am I saying? - we're on the run. We'll just go and we'll buy whatever we need.

(They pause, staring at each other. Gradually, OLLIE slides down the bench and stops at the edge, face to face with SOPHIE. Slowly, they start to kiss, a small kiss at first and then it becomes a long, passionate embrace. After a moment they withdraw slightly, already younger, lighter, both smiling and perhaps giggling slightly.

Suddenly, offstage, we here a woman's voice calling out, "OLLIE ... OLLIE." OLLIE abruptly looks toward the exit and grabs SOPHIE)

SOPHIE: What? What is it?

OLLIE: That's her.

(Again we hear the woman's voice call out, "OLLIE.")

SOPHIE: Wait. You're OLLIE?

OLLIE: I am. (The woman's voice shouts, "OLLIE, where are you?") I don't know your name.

SOPHIE: Huh? Oh -I'm SOPHIE.

(The voice continues calling out "OLLIE ... OLLIE ... OLLIE," while SOPHIE and OLLIE cling to each other, becoming aware that they are trapped. After a moment, SOPHIE asks, trying to be lighthearted)

Is it short for Oliver? (OLLIE nods) It's a good name. (Again, offstage, "OLLIE." A long pause) I guess you should go.

(Suddenly, SOPHIE lets go of him. OLLIE pulls back slowly. SOPHIE lowers her head, no longer able to look at him. Methodically, OLLIE rises, walks past her and moves upstage. SOPHIE watches him walking away, but turns her head away when OLLIE stops before the exit. HE turns, pausing, and stares downstage toward SOPHIE. The lights dim)

CURTAIN.

About Redburn Press

This is the first Redburn Press title. Redburn Press gets its name from the early Melville novel. In it, the autobiographical narrator goes to sea for the first time excitedly. The ship is full of fascinating types, eccentric human nature in its motley richness. And Wellingborough Redburn then encounters more "life and life only".

I want Redburn Press to be that ship in a bottle, so to speak. I want to publish eclectic, various, good books full of life. Google Redburn Press or go to markkohut.com to find other Redburn titles.

Mark Kohut

www.ingramcontent.com/pod-product-compliance
Lightning Source LLC
Chambersburg PA
CBHW051717040426
42446CB00008B/929